Praise 1

M000280242

"Susan Scott does a superb job of teaching couples how to create compelling conversations and foster true connection and a fierce love that will withstand the test of time and grow stronger over the years. Every couple should read this book!"

> —Marshall Goldsmith, *New York Times* #1
> bestselling author of *Triggers*, *Mojo*, and
> *What Got You Here Won't Get You There*

"In *Fierce Love*, Susan Scott creates a brilliant yet simple guide that inspires, and frames the most important conversations necessary to create understanding, empathy, and connection between two people. These are the tools to create deep and enduring relationships that last!"

> —Gregory Dickow, senior pastor of
> Life Changers International Church

"Love is often expressed sentimentally and romantically. In *Fierce Love*, Susan Scott offers a pungent vision of love as a real conversation between two authentic people with no topic off the table. After identifying the myths of love, she offers a model, and a list of the conversations authentic lovers should have. Bereft of romanticism and filled with directness, this book will help any couple live their relationship in a different way. We recommend it to all couples who want to move from good to great."

> —Harville Hendrix and Helen LaKelly Hunt, authors of
> *Getting the Love You Want: A Guide for Couples*

"In *Fierce Love*, Susan Scott candidly addresses an issue that commonly plagues many of our romantic relationships: lack of deep, vulnerable, and honest conversations. With compelling narrative and actionable steps, Scott helps readers harness the power of meaningful conversations to transform guarded love into fearless love that will unite couples for the long haul."

—Jenny Albers, author of *Courageously Expecting*

"Our relationships, our family, can and should be our biggest gift, even though I'm often tempted to treat them as my biggest pain in the butt. Susan Scott teaches us how to fight for this love—gently but fiercely—as imperfect but perfectly lovable beings."

—Anna Lind Thomas, author of *We'll Laugh About This Someday*

"In a time where many people are struggling with their relationships, we need voices that provide us with the courage, clarity, and skill to nurture our relationships and resolve recurring issues. Whether we are married or dating, we all need to have the conversations that may have eluded us. As I often say, in order for us to be great at anything, we need instruction. Susan Scott provides the necessary instruction while serving as a sisterly friend, with a great sense of humor, who helps us connect with our intimate partners at a deep level."

—Dondré Whitfield, actor and author of *Male vs. Man*

fierce

love

a journal for couples

Also by Susan Scott

Fierce Love: Creating a Love that Lasts—
One Conversation at a Time
Fierce Leadership: A Bold Alternative to the
Worst "Best" Practices of Business Today
Fierce Conversations: Achieving Success at Work
& in Life, One Conversation at a Time

fierce

love

a journal for couples

8 conversations to a
happier, healthier relationship

susan scott

New York Times Bestselling Author

NELSON
BOOKS

An Imprint of Thomas Nelson

Fierce Love: A Journal for Couples

© 2022 Susan Scott

All rights reserved. No portion of this book may be reproduced, stored in a retrieval system, or transmitted in any form or by any means—electronic, mechanical, photocopy, recording, scanning, or other—except for brief quotations in critical reviews or articles, without the prior written permission of the publisher.

Published in Nashville, Tennessee, by Nelson Books, an imprint of Thomas Nelson. Nelson Books and Thomas Nelson are registered trademarks of HarperCollins Christian Publishing, Inc.

Thomas Nelson titles may be purchased in bulk for educational, business, fundraising, or sales promotional use. For information, please e-mail SpecialMarkets@ThomasNelson.com.

Any internet addresses, phone numbers, or company or product information printed in this book are offered as a resource and are not intended in any way to be or to imply an endorsement by Thomas Nelson, nor does Thomas Nelson vouch for the existence, content, or services of these sites, phone numbers, companies, or products beyond the life of this book.

Portions of the text in *Fierce Love: A Journal for Couples* have been taken from *Fierce Love*.

Library of Congress Cataloging-in-Publication Data

Names: Scott, Susan, 1944- author.
Title: Fierce love: a journal for couples : 8 conversations to a happier, healthier relationship / Susan Scott.
Description: Nashville, Tennessee : Nelson Books, [2022] | Summary: "In this guided journal, New York Times bestselling author Susan Scott leads couples through eight must-have conversations to create a fierce love that stands the test of time and grows stronger over the years"--Provided by publisher.
Identifiers: LCCN 2021041775 | ISBN 9781400234363 (trade paperback)
Subjects: LCSH: Couples--Psychology. | Intimacy (Psychology) | Love. | Interpersonal communication
Classification: LCC HQ801 .S36 2022 | DDC 302.34/6--dc23
LC record available at https://lccn.loc.gov/2021041775

Printed in the United States of America

22 23 24 25 26   LSC   10 9 8 7 6 5 4 3 2 1

When I pick up a book, I flip to the dedication,
which is always to someone else and not to me.
Not this book. This one's for you if you love and
are not loved, if you are loved and do not love, if
you don't love and are not loved (you're breaking
my heart), and if you love and are loved, which
of course is the ultimate experience we all want to
have. I hope this book will help you get there.

With you know what,
Susan Scott
September 2021

Contents

Contents

Part 3: The Eight Conversations of Fierce Love

Introduction

I've got some good news to share with you:
how much love you have is up to you.

If you're learning this for the first time, I'm excited for what may be in store for you. Being a loving and lovable human being begins with the conversations you have. When you choose to embrace honest, courageous, and meaningful conversations with your partner, you nurture a fierce love that lasts.

Of course, every authentic relationship will have tough moments. Yet if you're committed to nurturing meaningful conversations, that's where the magic can happen. As you work through this journal, you have the opportunity to improve your primary relationship by fostering conversations that will strengthen it.

A successful relationship between two people

doesn't hinge on luck or fate or good fortune or any other uncontrollable force. It actually depends on one thing: the conversations between them. Whether you want to learn how to love each other well for the first time or you used to love each other and want to get it back or you want to enrich an already-healthy relationship, this journal will help you implement what you learned in *Fierce Love* in your own life.

As you reflect on the ways you relate to others, perhaps you'll notice ways you've already been communicating well. And you might begin to notice areas of conversation where you've been failing miserably. Both of those are opportunities to nurture and enrich your relationship. While you'll likely still disagree with your partner sometimes, you'll have the tools you need to do it better.

Whether your relationship needs a good cleansing and a fresh coat of paint or a major renovation, today you can begin to take small steps that, in time, will get the job done.

Reflecting on yourself and your relationship in these pages is the place to start, but it's not the place to stop. You'll gain real traction when you choose to *practice* the kinds of conversations that will change your relationship. When you choose to show up authentically, day by day, hour by hour, you can experience fierce, enduring love, one conversation at a time.

In each chapter of *Fierce Love*, you likely considered some big, new, meaty ideas. And if you tried to power through the book, or try to power through this journal, you're at risk of poor digestion. So be kind to yourself. Take your time. If you stumble upon an idea or exercise that seems particularly meaningful or important to you, pause there. Camp out and take all the time you need.

The first ten chapters will help you process the idea of fierce love and the myths that can interfere with it. I hope you'll spend time reflecting on what each looks like in your own life. The next eight chapters are meant to equip you for eight fierce conversations you can engage in with your partner. And the final chapters will help you to synthesize what you're discovering.

My hope for you as you spend time in this journal is that you will choose to create love today. On purpose.

With fierce affection,
Susan Scott

PART 1

The Idea of
Fierce Love

1

The Conversation *Is* the Relationship

I can see it clearly. The moment the proverbial light bulb came on for me was when poet and author David Whyte shared at a conference about the relational insight of a young newlywed man: "The conversation *is* the relationship." This simple idea changed the game for me. Once I heard it, I couldn't imagine how I'd missed it. The epiphany helped me to understand the end of my own marriage, and it was also this seed that had been planted in my heart that would continue to grow and flourish and, one day, help others.

If we agree that the conversation *is* the relationship, then the quality of the conversation gives us important clues to the quality of the relationship. Which of these indicators can you identify in your relationship today?

☐ We don't talk as much as we used to.
☐ Our conversations aren't as *robust* as they once were.
☐ I, or we, avoid upsetting topics.
☐ I, or we, offer or accept comments or behavior that are hurtful.
☐ We no longer aim for harmony or understanding.
☐ We tolerate a kind of deafness to one another.

Do you recognize any other indicators in your conversations that point to signs of sickness in the relationship? What are they?

_____

_____

_____

_____

TOPICS WE CAN'T DISCUSS

Maybe you've realized that you can no longer discuss her mother's alcoholism. Or you avoid mentioning anything related to his gambling. Or perhaps you've both stopped talking about sex. Or the subject you avoid may be as benign as yard work! You've each learned that, in order to keep a deathly peace, you will steer clear of certain topics.

What are the topics in your relationship that you and your partner avoid?

I avoid discussing . . . _____

_____

My partner avoids discussing . . . _____

We avoid discussing . . . _____

CHOOSING FIERCE CONVERSATIONS

A fierce conversation is one in which we come out from behind ourselves, into the conversation, and make it real. Rather than dodging hot topics, we are bold to say what we really think and feel. We choose to show up truthfully.

How are you feeling as you consider this possibility of showing up to every conversation truthfully?

_____

_____

What do you fear? What would be the worst thing that could happen? Be specific.

_____

_____

WHAT IT LOOKS
LIKE TO BE REAL

Being real doesn't mean vomiting every thought that's ever passed through your mind onto an unsuspecting other. Fierce conversations do, however, require emotional honesty. As you read through a few markers of emotional honesty below, identify which ones feel *easy* and which ones feel *difficult*.

Easy / Difficult   I tell my partner how I feel in the moment.

Easy / Difficult   I tell my partner when he or she has said or done something that hurts me.

Easy / Difficult   I tell my partner when he or she has warmed my heart, making me feel closer to him or her.

For one that was easy, describe the last time you did this.

_____

_____

For one that was difficult, write down the words you could say, in the future, to communicate well with your partner.

_____

_____

Note: Sometimes it's hard to practice new skills in the midst of a tricky conversation. So take the opportunity to journal the *kinds* of healthy dialogue you'd like to be able to share in conversation.

WHAT'S WRONG WITH CAREFUL CONVERSATIONS

When we engage in "careful" conversations, we tiptoe so as not to upset our partners. But careful conversations are failed conversations because they simply *postpone* the conversation that wants and needs to take place.

We may say that we're being careful so as not to hurt the other. But this can be a convenient excuse for our own cowardice! The alternative—and what may actually be less hurtful than the tiptoeing—is to address the issue in a way that will enrich your relationship.

Can you identify recent—or not-so-recent—conversations where you've danced around an issue, rather than address it directly, so as "not to hurt the other person"?

_____

_____

What was the result?

_____

_____

What would have been a bold, truthful way to have that conversation?

_____

_____

KEEPING IT REAL

Even when we've committed ourselves to living authentically, execution takes courage. For many of us, it's natural to project images we imagine others desire. Whether it's our home décor, the cars we drive, the clothes we buy, the makeup we wear, or the conversations we have, we may—wittingly or unwittingly—be presenting an unreal image of how we want others to view us.

Authenticity isn't something we have; it's something we choose. In each moment we have the opportunity to let others see who we really are or to mask up. And when we choose to come out from behind the mask by abandoning what's unreal, we move toward what we really want: happier relationships, personal freedom, and a life that fits us better.

As you consider the ways you present yourself to the world—to your partner, your family, your friends, and others—can you identify places where you'd prefer for others to see someone *other* than who you really are? (*Note:* You'll glean the most value from this exercise if you can be as honest as possible with yourself. Take your time. Pause for reflection. Be brave.)

_____

_____

_____

ONE THING

What is the one thing in this chapter that is most meaningful for you today? What idea or practice has the most traction in your life right now?

_____

_____

JUST DO IT

What is your next step? What is one practical way that you will implement this meaningful idea or practice in your life this week?

_____

_____

2

Gradually Then Suddenly

When we look at some of the big events and seasons of our lives—the graduation, the marriage, the divorce, the business merger, the addiction—we might naturally ask, "How did I get here?" And like Hemingway's character in *The Sun Also Rises*, we may answer, "Gradually and then suddenly." Often in hindsight we can search back through our history and recognize the important conversations—or missed conversations—that set things in motion.

The twenty-year marriage of a woman I know ended

suddenly when her husband, who'd been a pastor, came out as being gay. That was the conversation that set events in motion. Yet when they began to unpack those two decades with a therapist, the husband reminded his wife, "Remember when we were dating? I said that I thought I might be gay. And you said, 'Of course you're not gay.'" That was a brief conversation that the wife had "missed," as did her husband, as being pretty vital! They also recalled failed conversations about sex, where they felt stuck. And conversations along the way that they should have had but did not.

As we become more aware, we can learn to notice the "graduallys" that add up to a "suddenly."

FAILED CONVERSATIONS, MISSING CONVERSATIONS, AND THE CONVERSATIONS WE MISSED

Often when something happens suddenly, we can look at the evidence and return to conversations to see the ways it was happening gradually. We notice the conversations that set things in motion, the ones we missed, the ones that failed, and the ones we should have had.

failed or missed conversations

As you consider your primary relationship today and

the key issues you're facing together, consider the conversations you've had over the course of your relationship.

WHAT WERE THE CONVERSATIONS THAT SET EVENTS IN MOTION? These are the pivotal conversations you remember because they changed the game. They're the ones that led directly to a "suddenly." After these conversations everything was different.

_____

_____

_____

WHAT WERE THE CONVERSATIONS YOU MISSED? Like the woman whose husband came out as being gay, can you recognize a hint of a conversation that should have happened between you but did not? Maybe something taboo, a subject you were hesitant to broach?

_____

_____

_____

WHAT WERE THE FAILED CONVERSATIONS? These are conversations where you tried but were stuck. They were the conversations where you didn't fight fair. They were frustrating and felt hopeless. They weren't fruitful.

_____

_____

_____

RECOGNIZING YOUR "GRADUALLYS"

When our relationships begin to fail, we may not even notice at first. She begins coming home later and later from work. He becomes increasingly engaged with someone he's texting. She starts to confide primarily in friends rather than in him. He gradually stops initiating sex. The credit card bills escalate, and you can barely pay the minimum. You're worried about your financial future.

As you think of an area where you and your partner are stuck today, pause to consider the signs—the "graduallys"—that may be clues from while you were sleeping to the reality you're waking up to today. Be gentle and kind with yourself as you do.

Looking back, what "graduallys" do you recognize today?

_____

_____

BEING AWAKE

In "A Ritual to Read to Each Other," former poet laureate William Stafford wrote, "It is important that awake people be awake." (Everyone wakes up at "suddenly.") Maybe your "suddenly" has already happened. Or maybe you feel like your relationship has been gradually decaying but there is room to grow and improve.

Are you able to notice the ways that you have fostered or *allowed* gradual shifts to occur in your relationship? Maybe when your partner stopped initiating sex, you also silently agreed to avoid intimacy. Or perhaps you avoided conversations about the pills she takes because it was easier than having the hard conversations.

Noticing your own complicity, what are the
specific ways in which you've *allowed* gradual
shifts in your relationship?

_____

_____

YOUR "HERE"

Think about where you are today, your "here." "Here"
is the relational space in which you find yourself today.

What words or phrases describe your most
important relationship right now, or a relationship
that ended?

_____

_____

_____

YOUR "THERE"

Now imagine where you want to be, your "there." This is the relationship you desire. What words or phrases describe that relationship?

_____

_____

"HERE" TO "THERE"

Sometimes the distance between "here" and "there" isn't far at all. Other times it seems so great as to be unattainable. And sometimes you will be surprised that the destination that felt far off is actually easily traversable. The way people in relationship get from "here" to "there" is always the same: _by engaging in fierce conversations._ When partners are real, when they show up authentically, when they speak truthfully, they can get to their "there."

Say something about the gap that you perceive today between your "here" and your "there."

From where you sit today, does the journey feel possible? Why or why not?

_____

_____

ONE THING

What is the one thing in this chapter that is most meaningful for you today? What idea or practice has the most traction in your life right now?

_____

_____

JUST DO IT

What is your next step? What is one practical way that you will implement this meaningful idea or practice in your life this week?

_____

_____

3

All Conversations
Are with Myself

Sasha and Darnell had been dating for three months. Within a few weeks of meeting, both had been "all in," and both assumed the relationship was heading toward marriage. However, Sasha started feeling anxious about the relationship. When she finally initiated the hard conversation, she suggested that they "slow things down." Darnell remained almost silent throughout the conversation/monologue. When Sasha asked for his thoughts, he said, "I feel so rejected. I'm out."

Sasha felt confused because she hadn't intended

to reject him. She hadn't wanted to break up. She'd expected him to agree that nothing was being lost by slowing down and that their relationship might actually end up stronger for it. It was as if she and Darnell had been in different conversations altogether.

THE STORIES WE TELL

Darnell had told himself a story that wasn't true. A lot of us do. A woman who was adopted out of foster care may falsely believe she is "damaged goods." A man who never knew his father may believe he's "not worth loving." Someone who has been abandoned may believe that "everybody leaves." A woman may be concerned about aging because she believes that her physical attractiveness is all she has to offer.

Based on what we've experienced, we tell ourselves stories that aren't true. Sometimes, rejection by a parent becomes the story we tell. Or the story might be, "Conflict means the relationship ends." It's not always easy to recognize the old stories we project onto current relationships. And yet when we pull back the curtain, we can expose the harmful stories we've told and embrace those that are *more true*.

As you consider the patterns in the relationships in your life, do you recognize a "story" you've carried, a belief that hasn't served you, that has hindered you from being in the present? What is the story?

_____

_____

_____

What did you believe that story said about who you are?

_____

_____

WHAT I BELIEVE, WHAT I DO, WHAT I GET

What we believe is inextricably bound to what we do and what results from what we do.

Jamie grew up in a household where she was physically abused. As a result, she naturally developed the belief, "I'm not worth protecting." She ended up dating a man who also treated her poorly. And because she believed, in her deep places, that she wasn't worth protecting, she stayed in the relationship longer than she should have.

As you consider the old, stale belief you've been hauling around, what results has that belief produced in your life?

_____

_____

How has that belief been harmful to your relationships?

_____

_____

DOING IT DIFFERENTLY

As long as we're being bullied by the old belief, we'll keep getting what we've always gotten. But once that old belief is exposed, we can finally replace it with something that is more true.

Jamie believed, "I'm not worth protecting."

WHAT IS MORE TRUE: "Although I've been hurt in the past, I'm actually precious, and I'm worth protecting."

The person who's been abandoned believes, "I'm not worth sticking around for."

WHAT IS MORE TRUE: "Although others have left me, I'm actually worth loving."

The child who is sent to foster care may believe, "I'm damaged. I'm unlovable."

WHAT IS MORE TRUE: "Although others have failed to love me well, I am valuable, and I am worth loving."

As you consider the lie you've been told, the story you've believed, what is *more true*? (*Note:* It may not be easy for you to get at this. What would you say to a precious child who is carrying this poisonous belief?)

_____

_____

_____

_____

_____

WHAT YOU *REALLY* BELIEVE

Consider this chart from *Fierce Love* and check the beliefs you hold. Don't check what you think you ought to check. Check the beliefs that you *really* hold. There will likely be checks in both columns.

I BELIEVE

☐ Disclosing my real thoughts and feelings is risky.	☐ Disclosing what I really think and feel frees up energy and expands possibilities.
☐ My partner can't handle the truth, so it's better not to say anything.	☐ Though I have trouble handling the truth sometimes, I'll keep telling it and inviting it from my partner.
☐ It's important that I convince my partner that my point of view is correct.	☐ Exploring my partner's point of view will lead to better decisions for both of us.

☐ I will gain approval and affection by exchanging my authentic self for the image I imagine my partner desires.	☐ My authentic self will be expanded as my partner gets to know and love the real me.
☐ Reality can't be changed. There's no point in fighting it.	☐ Perhaps we can change reality with thoughtful conversations.
☐ The best way to support my partner is to give advice.	☐ The best way to support my partner is to ask questions that help him/ her gain insight into what needs to happen.
☐ I'll keep my mouth shut. My partner probably knows best.	☐ My point of view is as valid as my partner's.
☐ I need to ignore what I'm feeling in my gut; just put my head down and pretend everything is okay.	☐ I know what I know, and what I know, I need to act on.

What did you learn from this exercise? Did anything surprise you?

_____

_____

_____

_____

BELIEF, BEHAVIOR, RESULT

In addition to believing what is damaging and false about ourselves, we may also carry false beliefs about our partners. For instance, we might quietly believe that he or she isn't smart, isn't capable, isn't worthy, isn't lovable, isn't [fill in the blank].

Take a moment to interrogate the wizard behind the curtain who is running your life. Write down two beliefs you currently hold about yourself and your partner that could be damaging your relationship. For example, "I believe I'm physically unattractive, so I avoid physical intimacy with my spouse. As a result, our relationship suffers."

Belief about myself: _____

Behavior: _____

Result: _____

Belief about my partner: _____

Behavior: _____

Result: _____

Expose more beliefs, and explore these possibilities further, by using a separate sheet of paper.

ONE THING

What is the one thing in this chapter that is most meaningful for you today? What idea or practice has the most traction in your life right now?

_____

_____

JUST DO IT

What is your next step? What is one practical way that you will implement this meaningful idea or practice in your life this week?

_____

_____

4

Crossing the
Bold Line

Magazine founder and editor Margaret Anderson's explanation of love resonates with me: "In real love you want the other person's good. In romantic love you want the other person." Our culture's Hollywood version of romantic love is iconic. Whether it's the Disney films we're fed as children, rom-coms starring Tom Hanks and Meg Ryan, or modern films' quick hookup stories that turn out to be "true love," these stories feed our imaginations and cause us to believe that falling in love is all about our own happiness.

RELATIONSHIPS ARE LIVING THINGS

Relationships are living, breathing things with a pulse, needs, and a purpose. This means that we have to be actively feeding the relationship for it to be sustained, let alone grow. Investing in the relationship and each other takes intention.

In what ways in your relationship, today, do you seek the good of and for your partner?

_____

_____

_____

In what ways in your relationship, today, do you seek your own good?

_____

_____

_____

CAREFUL RELATIONSHIPS
VERSUS FIERCE ONES

The careful couple pretends it's all good until their relationship "suddenly" explodes. These couples are more concerned with how they look from the outside than with what is happening on the inside. Concerned with what others might think, they hide whatever might displease or alarm others.

The fiercely passionate couple, however, is committed to fierce conversations. Fierce love. Fierce commitment. Fierce satisfaction. Partners feel safe to be the unique persons they are and safe to take a stand for what each believes in and desires.

The rub is often that we want the benefits of fierceness without the discomfort that's often required to keep fierceness alive.

Pause to notice the vibrancy of your relationship.

In what ways is your relationship careful?

_____

_____

_____

In what ways is your relationship fierce?

_____

_____

_____

THE THREAT OF FEAR

What keeps us from daring to be authentic, and thus producing a fierce relationship, is fear. When we are bossed around by fear, we avoid what we don't want, but we fail to move toward what we do want. In a fierce relationship you face your fears. In a careful relationship you hide from them.

Where do you see fear meddling in your relationship today?

_____

_____

_____

LOVE VERSUS FIERCE LOVE

Are you ready to take your love to another level? Are you prepared to love boldly, intimately, fiercely? Do you want to experience a deeper connection? Why or why not?

_____

_____

_____

_____

Describe the type of relationship you hope to experience with your partner.

_____

_____

_____

_____

FIERCE CONVERSATIONS
AS CAMPFIRES

What qualities of fierce love can you recognize, today, in your relationship? If the fire is not raging, can you remember a moment when this spark of fierce love was present in your relationship?

_____

_____

Put a check beside each fierce quality you recognize in your relationship today. Then, beside each, list a specific example from your relationship. (For example: conversation in car on the way home from in-laws' anniversary party, his enthusiasm for my promotion, etc.)

Fierce love . . .
- ☐ is passionate,
- ☐ is authentic,
- ☐ is courageous,
- ☐ nurtures connection,
- ☐ is rational and emotional,
- ☐ invites radical transparency,

☐ lends small gestures great importance,

☐ is assured and unselfconscious,

☐ desires and values,

☐ exists between equal partners,

☐ is sustainable and subtle,

☐ is interesting and unadorned,

☐ often defers,

☐ evokes home and supports the complexity of relationships,

☐ values relationship over things,

☐ doesn't always agree but always understands, and

☐ overlooks small imperfections.

Pause to spend time noticing these sparks, from the present and the past, that kindle fierce love in your relationship.

CHOOSING A FIERCE LOVE

Here are some transformations and characteristics of fierce love. After each pairing, jot down a few notes about *what you are seeing in your relationship today* and where you'd like to grow.

Before Fierce Love: Settling for mediocrity, maintaining the illusion that everything is okay

Practicing Fierce Love: Consciously nurturing love every day, keeping it real

---

Before Fierce Love: Hoping and trying to change your partner, believing he or she is the problem

Practicing Fierce Love: Working on yourself, embracing accountability

---

Before Fierce Love: Me-versus-you relationship—it's all about me

Practicing Fierce Love: Partnership and mutuality—what can I do to support you?

Before Fierce Love: Low engagement, nothing changes

Practicing Fierce Love: Identifying the issues at the heart of your relationship, generating impetus for change

---

Before Fierce Love: Blaming—entrenched victim mode

Practicing Fierce Love: Deep-seated accountability—seeing where I contributed to this problem

---

Before Fierce Love: No shared vision or values, competing goals

Practicing Fierce Love: Shared vision and values, taking next steps together

---

Before Fierce Love: High level of dissatisfaction, difficulty maintaining intimacy

Practicing Fierce Love: Both people feeling seen and heard, increased intimacy

---

Before Fierce Love: Stalled personal growth, individual stagnation

Practicing Fierce Love: Shared enthusiasm for personal growth, shared responsibility for kindling the relationship

---

Before Fierce Love: Sex is rare, rote, selfish, quick, lacking intimacy

Practicing Fierce Love: Lovemaking is spontaneous, generous, honest, connection building

---

ONE THING

What is the one thing in this chapter that is most meaningful for you today? What idea or practice has the most traction in your life right now?

_____

_____

JUST DO IT

What is your next step? What is one practical way that you will implement this meaningful idea or practice in your life this week?

_____

_____

5

What *Isn't* Fierce Love?

In a lot of our lives, no one ever taught us to trust our gut. Likely no parent showed us how to look inside and notice what our heart was telling us. They didn't coach us, "When someone does or says something that doesn't feel right and your instincts tell you something is up, you're right: it is."

So, left to our own devices, we chose to remain blind to what we didn't want to see, deaf to what we didn't want to hear. To our detriment, many of us became experts at it.

YOU CAN'T CHANGE PEOPLE

If we see it as a slogan emblazoned on a T-shirt—"You Can't Change People"—or as a carefully embroidered sentiment on a pillow, we smile and nod and politely agree that we can't change other people. But when it comes to our relationships, it may be another story entirely. While we might not ever *consciously* tell ourselves that we can change others, we quietly live as if it's true. We overlook a potentially disastrous flaw. We turn away from that thing that is actually pretty problematic. And although we may not willfully believe that we can change people, we can be very creative about imagining the ways they are, or can be, different than they actually are.

At the beginning of your relationship, was there a way in which you hoped or believed someone would change and be other than they were? (*Note:* At first it may have been a little endearing, but eventually it has become maddening.)

_____

_____

How has that worked out for you in your relationship?

_____

_____

WHEN THINGS DON'T ADD UP

He began spending more time with women at work. One invited him out to see a show. He'd been irritable with his wife, Scarlet. And she sensed that although she couldn't put her finger on it, something was *off*. It wasn't until she discovered the sexually explicit emails between her husband and a female coworker that Scarlet was able to know, definitely, that things weren't adding up. But a part of her *had* wondered. And perhaps a part of her *did* know. When we're avoiding fiercely honest conversations, we aren't dealing with what's really going on.

Are there any signs in your relationship, today, that you've been ignoring? What are they?

_____

_____

READ THE SIGNS

A neighbor has mentioned to you that she notices your husband drinking liquor in the garage when he's grilling. A single friend saw your serious girlfriend on a dating website. A friend from church innocently reported seeing your spouse out at a fancy restaurant, in a neighboring town, with someone who wasn't you. Often the paths of our relationships have been littered with warning signs that we've ignored.

There are four conversational signs that were identified by the Gottman Institute that could predict, with over 90 percent accuracy, whether or not a couple would divorce: criticism, defensiveness, contempt, and stonewalling.

As you think about recent conversations with your partner, do you notice any of these warning signs in the way the two of you relate? It might be your partner, and it might be you! With a spirit of humility and honesty, note specific examples, from particular conversations, in which you can recognize one of these:

Criticism

Defensiveness

_____

_____

Contempt

_____

_____

Stonewalling

_____

_____

WITHHOLDING

Although I'm never surprised anymore when people tell me why they didn't say what they wanted to say to their partner, I'm still often alarmed by some of the admissions I hear.

Can you recall a recent conversation (or conversations)

45

when there was something that you held back from your partner? Use the exercise below to help you recall what was at work inside you when you chose not to say something to your partner:

I didn't say . . . _____

Because . . . _____

I didn't say . . . _____

Because . . . _____

I didn't say . . . _____

Because . . . _____

As you recall how the conversation unfolded, what might have been different if you'd shared honestly about what was on your mind?

_____

_____

_____

READ THE SIGNS

In *Fierce Love,* I shared some signs that might signal that you are heading toward an unpleasant "suddenly." If you need a refresher on what expressions of each look like, peek back at chapter 5. Check the box beside each that has marked your recent conversations:

- ☐ Conflict avoidance
- ☐ Dishonest conversations
- ☐ Triangulating
- ☐ Lack of honest feedback
- ☐ Failure to tell your partner how much they are appreciated
- ☐ Withholding your frustration
- ☐ Allowing the relationship to flatline
- ☐ Prolonged silence
- ☐ Living with fear
- ☐ Not enjoying physical intimacy
- ☐ Failing to grow personally, to adjust, to change as needed
- ☐ Allowing your relationship to be at risk

Which of the signs you checked is the most detrimental to your relationship today? In what specific instance did you and your partner last experience it? Discuss this with your partner.

_____

_____

_____

THAT'S WHAT I FEEL TOO!

We know the types of topics that people usually refrain from bringing up in polite company:

- That time my husband had an affair
- When I was molested as a child
- The embarrassing medical condition I live with
- That thing I did that I'm ashamed to admit

And yet when we hear someone who is living authentically, who is courageous enough to broach a tricky topic in an appropriate setting, it feels amazing, doesn't it? We discover that we are not alone, and we want to throw up our arms and yell, "Yes, yes, yes, that is exactly what I feel too!"

Can you remember a moment when you were in a space where someone's vulnerable sharing was what you most needed to hear? Do you remember how it set part of you free? Journal a bit about that experience.

_____

_____

_____

ONE THING

What is the one thing in this chapter that is most meaningful for you today? What idea or practice has the most traction in your life right now?

_____

_____

JUST DO IT

What is your next step? What is one practical way that you will implement this meaningful idea or practice in your life this week?

_____

_____

PART 2

The Five Myths That Mislead and Derail Us

6

Myth 1: You Complete Me

A friend in her early fifties has dipped her toe into the world of online dating. She reports that men's profiles reveal more about them than they likely realize (women's too!). One man shares about his rich, full life and how he'd enjoy sharing it with someone. This, she tells me, is appealing. Another man, however, wrote just six words: "Looking for someone to complete me." In the world of online dating, and in the world *outside* of online dating, this is called a "red flag." It signals *caution*. The best relationships aren't ones in which partial humans find someone who they believe will make them whole; the best relationships are ones in which whole humans have met other whole humans with whom they can create fierce love.

BEING ENMESHED

It's likely you know a person, or a couple, who is easily "enmeshed." They end up in relationships that they hope will *complete* them.

Who do you know who is like this?

_____

_____

As you consider these types of relationships, what is lost when each individual isn't thriving as a unique individual? What have you seen a loved one sacrifice that should have been preserved and protected?

_____

_____

ADDING OR SUBTRACTING

In chapter 6 I shared the story of a young woman we called Kate. The gist of Kate's story is that she exchanged her full, robust life for a lesser one when she began dating. Though her significant other didn't ask it of her, Kate gradually forfeited parts of her life that had previously been meaningful. In this kind of situation, *everyone* loses. Conversely, the person who is committed to his or her own flourishing is looking to be in a relationship that doesn't diminish who he or she is but instead supports his or her flourishing.

Think back to the beginning of your relationship with your partner. To the best of your ability, try to remember:

What were the ways in which being in a relationship with this person inspired you to be *more* of the flourishing person you were made to be?

_____

_____

_____

What were the ways in which being in a relationship with this person caused you to be *less* of the flourishing person you were made to be?

_____

_____

As you consider the things you sacrificed, are you able to take responsibility for those choices? Specifically, what was your part?

_____

_____

FIRST THINGS FIRST

Before you can know whether or not you want to be in a particular relationship, there's a question you need to answer: *Is my life working for me?* If a relationship is going to work, it needs to be between two authentic people who are living as who they really are.

Setting aside your relationship, or hope of a relationship, pause to consider whether or not the life you have is working for you right now.

On a scale of 1 to 10, rate each area of your life, and note why you chose that score:

WORK LIFE

1   2   3   4   5   6   7   8   9   10

FRIENDSHIPS

1   2   3   4   5   6   7   8   9   10

FAMILY RELATIONSHIPS

1   2   3   4   5   6   7   8   9   10

PHYSICAL HEALTH

1   2   3   4   5   6   7   8   9   10

EMOTIONAL HEALTH

1   2   3   4   5   6   7   8   9   10

SPIRITUAL LIFE

1   2   3   4   5   6   7   8   9   10

Today, in which area or areas are you thriving?

_____

_____

Today, in which area or areas are you struggling?

_____

_____

Which area needs the most improvement?

_____

_____

THE REAL YOU

In various seasons of our lives—and ideally all of them!—we have opportunities to glimpse and lean into being the person we were made to be. Maybe we were enlivened by a service project during college. Perhaps we feel vivified spending time in the garden. Or we might feel fully alive when we're doing great work with a motivated team. We experience joy and satisfaction when we become that person we were designed to be and do those things we were designed to do.

Note: Spend some time with this. Don't rush. Sometimes it can help to think back through different seasons of your life.

When did you feel most fully alive? Happy in your own skin?

_____

_____

THE FALSE SELF

When we neglect our authentic selves, we trade our real selves for the selves we imagine others desire. When we go home we wear the outfit we know will make our mother smile. We even hang that horrible painting she gave us on the wall and put it back in the closet when she leaves. We do the job we are expected to do, and possibly even _trained_ to do, though our hearts lie elsewhere. We go out with the gang to parties and clubs when we're yearning to be curled up on the couch reading a book.

As you think about your life today, exclusive of your partner, notice the ways in which you are failing to be who you really are.

The last time I masked up to pretend to be someone I was not . . .

_____

_____

The last time I agreed to do something I'd prefer not to do . . .

_____

_____

The last time I catered to who I thought someone else wanted me to be . . .

_____

_____

The last time I acted in a way that wasn't authentic . . .

_____

_____

The last time I tried to be like somebody else . . .

_____

_____

The last time I compromised who I am . . .

_____

_____

KEEPING IT REAL

As you consider the ways that you've failed to be who you really are and strive to live authentically, what is the immediate growing edge in your life? What is an area in which you see room for growth?

_____

_____

What will you do differently in this area?

_____

_____

_____

ONE THING

What is the one thing in this chapter that is most meaningful for you today? What idea or practice has the most traction in your life right now?

_____

_____

JUST DO IT

What is your next step? What is one practical way that you will implement this meaningful idea or practice in your life this week?

_____

_____

7

Myth 2: True Love Is Unconditional

At one level, unconditional love is the thing for which we all hunger. So I understand the appeal. But when we're able to release the fantasy of an unconditional love that fixes all mistakes, overlooks all wrongs, or heals all wounds—which, to be clear, it does not—we'll actually be able to love one another *better*.

WE TEACH OTHERS
HOW TO TREAT US

In all of our relationships, we teach others how to treat us. If we allow a boss's cruel, jagged criticism with no resistance, we're teaching that boss that it's permissible to treat us that way. If a neighbor consistently throws his trash in our garbage bin so that he never has to drag his to the curb and we never speak up, we've taught him to treat us that way. And in our most intimate relationships, we teach others how to treat us when we allow their bad behavior toward us.

In what way or ways have you taught your partner to treat you poorly? What behavior have you allowed that taught that to him or her?

_____

_____

_____

_____

WE GET WHAT WE TOLERATE

Remember Roger and Lori from the deck of my tree house? When Lori got all googly-eyed and told Roger that there was nothing he could ever do that would cause her to leave him, she didn't quite realize the magnitude of what she was declaring. In essence, she was saying, "You can cheat on me again, and I won't leave you." And she was unwittingly also saying, "You can neglect me, abuse me, harm me, and more, and I won't leave you." That is where the "unconditional love" logic between two human beings leads. So we shouldn't be surprised when behavior that we've tolerated, and vowed to tolerate in the future, repeats itself.

Do you recognize any harmful patterns in your relationship because of a behavior you have tolerated, until now, without resistance?

_____

_____

_____

FORGIVENESS IS DIFFERENT FROM LOVE WITHOUT CONDITIONS

Does it feel to you as if this logic of "love with conditions" rubs against your convictions about loving relationships? Does it seem to run against your faith convictions? Consider that throughout the Bible, when a wrong is committed, it is not ignored. It is *named* as a wrong. Patterns of wrongdoing are named as *wrong.*

Because Lori was committed to her marriage, she chose to forgive Roger. I applaud her for that, and I saw the fruit it bore. But acknowledging a wrong and forgiving it is different from loving without conditions. When we're able to realistically acknowledge a wrong and the harm it has caused, and *then* forgive, we are building a stronger relationship than one in which we gloss over painful wrongs that have been committed.

Notice and name the offenses, the wrongs in your relationship that your partner has committed that you have glossed over, overlooked, or ignored. Be specific.

_____

_____

If you're willing to be brutally honest, are there offenses or wrongs in your relationship that you have committed that your partner has glossed over, overlooked, or ignored? Notice and name them.

_____

_____

_____

_____

LESSONS LEARNED FROM
THE GIVING TREE

Although I wasn't privy to every detail of Lori and Roger's relationship, what I know deeply is that unconditional love actually isn't the most loving option. A vivid expression of that is the relationship between a boy and a tree in Shel Silverstein's _The Giving Tree_. Twig by twig, branch by branch, limb by limb, the tree "gives itself" to the boy. (Please imagine me gesturing sarcastically with oversized air quotes.) How can a relationship be "loving" if one party is completely devastated by it?

As you think of relationships you've seen between couples you know well, can you think of one in which one party gave to the other to his or her detriment?

_____

_____

Why do you think he or she sacrificed in this way?

_____

_____

PREPARING TO HAVE THE CONVERSATION

Pause to consider your *personal* nonnegotiables that would cause you to step away from the relationship. Be kind to yourself in this process and take your time. Be careful not to be bullied by human voices and messages, even religious ones. When you hear those messages hissing in your ear—"A good wife never leaves" or "A husband loves unconditionally"—jot them down here, to expose them, and ask yourself what is *most* true. (In chapter 12 I'll give you guidelines for having this conversation, but for right now, spend some time in preparation.)

_____

_____

_____

What are your personal nonnegotiables that would cause you to step away from your relationship with your partner?

_____

_____

_____

REASONS OR RESULTS?

Have you ever told someone the ways that their behavior affected you and found their apology to be less than satisfying?

Fierce Love

"I yelled at you because I had a fight with my mom."

"I'm sorry I said you were incompetent. I'm just weary of . . ."

Apologies in which offenders offer reasons—excuses—for their behavior aren't as helpful as apologies in which the offenders take responsibility for the way they behaved.

On a scale of 1 to 10 (1 being "nonexistent" and 10 being "sincere"), my partner's apologies are a/an _____. And specific examples of recent conversations we've shared that caused me to choose this number are:

_____

_____

On a scale of 1 to 10 (1 being "nonexistent" and 10 being "sincere"), my *own* apologies are a/an _____. And specific examples of recent conversations we've shared that caused me to choose this number are:

_____

_____

Note: As you can imagine, you might not be the best judge of your own mastery of apologies. With a

70

willingness to learn and grow, invite your partner to offer his or her opinion on the rankings, as well as specific examples from recent conversations. This is fierce. And it's worth it.

ONE THING

What is the one thing in this chapter that is most meaningful for you today? What idea or practice has the most traction in your life right now?

_____

_____

JUST DO IT

What is your next step? What is one practical way that you will implement this meaningful idea or practice in your life this week?

_____

_____

8

Myth 3: You Must Fulfill My List

When we're dating, a lot of us have a list—
either explicit or hidden in our hearts—of the qualities
we're looking for in another. Perhaps we hope to find
someone who's tall, attractive, athletic, kind, generous,
faithful, wealthy, and who nurses sick puppies back
to health on the weekends. If people were robots and
could be created through a convenient online menu, that
combo might produce quite the remarkable human.

It turns out, however, that potential partners are not
robots. Just like us, they're a complicated combination

of nature and nurture. They've had a lifetime of unique experiences, as we have, that have contributed to making them the person you will meet at a coffee shop or on a dating site.

If you and I were friends and you showed me your long list of requirements for a significant other, I might accidentally-on-purpose laugh out loud. And when you were still looking for that special someone five years later, I'd ask, "So how's that list working out for you?"

NO ONE IS PERFECT

A friend of mine was dating a man long-distance. When their relationship got serious, he moved to the state in which she lived. Once they were living in the same city, she noticed a chronic quality in him that really irked her. (Imagine, here, something that would really get under your skin.) Should this be a deal breaker? Before their relationship went further, my friend needed to decide.

When you commit to someone, you commit to an imperfect person whose issues you'll be living with for a long time. Some are problems you can live with. Others may not be.

In theory, what behaviors in a partner would make the relationship intolerable?

_____

_____

If you're in a relationship today, what are the behaviors that you find most bothersome? How have you handled these?

_____

_____

THE OTHER PROBLEM WITH LISTS

Another problem with lists is that as we're eagerly scanning our prospects to see who checks the boxes, we may overlook an unlikely someone who'd be a great match for us. When people don't come in the packaging on our lists—whether it's appearance or income or education or something else entirely—we can easily be blinded and unable to recognize what's wonderful and remarkable about them.

If we overlook people with intellectual disabilities, we might miss out on a friend who's an amazing cook and host. If we fail to notice people who are older, we could miss out on a mentor who would add value to our lives. And if we have a long list of must-haves for the romantic relationship we hope to find, we might never find that perfect person who doesn't actually exist.

When in your life have you met an "unlikely someone" who surprisingly became someone you valued?

_____

_____

_____

What would you have missed out on if you'd overlooked him or her?

_____

_____

_____

DON'T BE HINDERED
BY YOUR LIST

Maybe you know a happy couple whose pairing surprises you. They might have very different body types, levels of education, hobbies, or bank accounts. And yet the couple that includes an unlikely someone is happy and their relationship is flourishing!

Who is one couple you know where one of the amazing partners is one you might not naturally have selected?

_____

_____

Name the areas where you could be more open to receiving those—either in significant relationships or friendships—who are different from you:

_____

_____

WHAT'S ON YOUR LIST?

You know how I feel about lists. But for the sake of this exercise, I'd love to hear what's on yours. What are the qualities you'd like to find in another? Don't be shy. Make it as robust as possible. (You'll thank me later.)

So what's on your list of qualities you hope to find in another? (Aim for at least ten! But go bigger if you're inspired.)

_____   _____

_____   _____

_____   _____

_____   _____

_____   _____

BE YOUR LIST

Now, in an exercise of brutal honesty, compare the list you made, above, to who *you* are today.

Which of those qualities are you living out?

_____

_____

Which of those qualities are you failing to live out?

_____

_____

I think you see where this is headed, right? You are the one who needs to embody the traits and characteristics you're looking for in others.

BE BETTER

How will you choose to embody the qualities on your list in which you are weak? The more specific you can be about the goal you want to achieve this week, the more likely you will be to accomplish it. For example, rather than saying "be nicer," you may want to make the goal measurable:

- I will invite my coworker Wanda to lunch.
- I'll visit my elderly neighbor one evening.
- I'll refrain from saying any unkind words about others.

What is one way, this week, that you can embody one of the qualities on your list in which you are weak?

_____

_____

ONE THING

What is the one thing in this chapter that is most meaningful for you today? What idea or practice has the most traction in your life right now?

_____

_____

JUST DO IT

What is your next step? What is one practical way that you will implement this meaningful idea or practice in your life this week?

_____

_____

9

Myth 4: If You Loved Me, You'd Know

Janet and Keisha hadn't seen each other for a year and were looking forward to getting together for lunch. They met up in a busy part of the city where they had lots of dining options.

"Where do you want to eat?" Keisha asked.

"Doesn't matter to me," Janet assured her. "Anything is good."

Keisha offered, "I've heard good things about Hutchins Pizza . . ."

"I'm lactose intolerant," Janet explained.

"Okay," Keisha continued. "How about Big Jim's Barbecue?"

"Sorry," Janet said. "I'm vegetarian."

"Alright," Keisha replied. "Is there a place you'd enjoy?"

"Gosh . . . really, anywhere," Janet said.

"There's a good Indian restaurant about a block from here," Keisha suggested.

"Ooh," Janet resisted, "just not my favorite . . ."

At the end of the painful process the pair eventually agreed on a restaurant with a salad bar and a variety of entrée options. But the journey to that decision was wearying. They could have landed there much sooner if Janet had been willing to say what she needed and wanted.

BEGIN TO NOTICE

We are so used to not saying what we're really thinking that we don't even catch ourselves in the act. Ostensibly we do it to preserve the bond we have with someone, fearing that any conflict might hinder our relationship. In fact, however, relationships are best served when we clearly articulate what we think, what we want, and what we need.

As you consider who you are in relationships, how easy or difficult is it for you to say what you're really thinking?

_____

_____

_____

With whom is it *most* easy? Why?

_____

_____

_____

With whom is it *most* difficult? Why?

_____

_____

_____

IF YOU LOVED ME . . .

If you kind of, sort of really hope that your significant other will magically read your mind and your heart and your body and know what you're thinking and feeling and wanting and needing, you're likely in for some major disappointment.

Pause to consider your relationship with your partner. Make a list of those moments when you failed to get what you needed from your partner because you didn't ask for it.

Maybe you wanted a hug.

Maybe your feelings were bruised.

Maybe you needed extra help with a household task.

Maybe you needed to hear the words "I love you."

What was the last encounter with your partner in which you didn't share what you were thinking or feeling and you were left feeling disappointed that your needs weren't met? What was that need?

_____

_____

_____

It can help to plan the words you'll use to share. What will you say next time?

_____

_____

_____

GOING BEYOND LOVE LANGUAGES

The five love languages offered in Gary Chapman's book _The Five Love Languages_ include words of affirmation, quality time, physical touch, acts of service, and receiving gifts. When you know your partner's particular love language, you're better able to speak it. You are able to love them in the way that they best receive love.

While these are truly valuable, there's more to a healthy relationship. And we really need that "more"—the ability to have fierce conversations—when we experience conflict or loneliness or disappointment with our partners. Because our partners aren't mind readers, we need to be able to tell them what we want and need at any given time.

Recall the last time that your partner was *not* caring for you in the ways you wanted and needed to be cared for. Were you able to stop for a moment and tell them?

_____

_____

If so, what was the response?

_____

_____

If not, what kept you from expressing yourself?

_____

_____

NOTICE THE "WHY"

For a lot of us, telling our partners what we want and need doesn't come naturally to us, especially if it wasn't modeled for us. If we didn't grow up seeing healthy people sharing what they were really thinking, it might naturally feel foreign. While it may feel awkward, finally saying what you really think and feel will benefit your current relationship.

As you think about the caregivers who shaped your early experience, did you hear adults saying what they were really thinking? Reflect on that, offering specific examples.

_____

_____

_____

Were you encouraged or discouraged from saying what you were really thinking? Reflect on that, offering specific examples.

_____

_____

_____

TELL ME!

Perhaps there's something you want or need today that you've not shared with your partner. Consider these possible conversations:

- Something I want is . . .
- Something I need is . . .
- I want you to do this . . .
- I want you to stop doing this . . .
- I'm upset with you because . . .
- I felt sad when you . . .
- When you did that, I felt . . .
- When you said [fill in the blank], I felt . . .
- I felt appreciated when you . . .

If you're not in the habit of saying what you're really thinking and feeling, beginning to have fierce conversations might feel a little scary. Know, though, that you have what it takes!

What is the conversation, today, that you need to have with your partner?

_____

_____

ONE THING

What is the one thing in this chapter that is most meaningful for you today? What idea or practice has the most traction in your life right now?

_____

_____

JUST DO IT

What is your next step? What is one practical way that you will implement this meaningful idea or practice in your life this week?

_____

_____

10

Myth 5: Love Is All You Need

When the Beatles sang "All You Need Is Love"—and beautifully, I might add—millions around the world felt inspired to believe that love can conquer any obstacle.

Ummm...

We go wrong when we think that love has limitless power, that it will provide what we don't even know we want. And we fool ourselves if we believe that we can love another through whatever character flaw they're displaying. *Even though loving someone won't necessarily change that person, our soul doesn't know this and persists in an impossible endeavor.* This is what twelve-steppers call "stinkin' thinkin'." Because as strong and mighty and noble and generous as our love for another may be, the other individual is actually the one who is responsible for his or her own growth.

LOVE MIGHT NOT BE ALL YOU NEED

While "love is all you need" might be a neat saying to emblazon on an inspirational T-shirt, the fact is that relationships need a little bit more than love.

As you think about your past relationships that have failed and those that have succeeded— both romantic ones and friendships—what, in your opinion, are the ingredients of a successful relationship?

_____

_____

_____

Which does your current relationship include?

_____

_____

Which is your current relationship lacking?

_____

_____

WHEN IT'S TIME TO LET GO

If you're like a lot of people I know, you take the "till death do us part" line of the wedding vows very seriously. You said that you would love your partner *no matter what*. And you would do it forever. Until death parts you.

Throughout the ages, across cultures, women and men who've entered into committed relationships have made the decision to end the relationships they hoped would flourish. People who have sought spiritual guidance, have made the hard decision to dissolve the union into which they entered. Maybe a spouse was chronically unfaithful. Or a significant other may have been physically or emotionally abusive to his or her partner or children. It may have become dangerous to live under the same roof with this person. And the most loving choice, considering all those involved, was to end the relationship.

Under what circumstances would you end a marriage to which you'd committed yourself for life? Why?

_____

_____

_____

CHOOSING TO END A RELATIONSHIP

Marriages aren't the only serious relationships where we invest our time and energy. And they aren't the only relationships that end. Sometimes we face a conflict with another person that feels insurmountable. A friend and business partner might feel he was robbed financially. A cousin might feel irreparably betrayed. A longtime friend from childhood does something that hurts us deeply. A child who was harmed by a parent may choose to sever the relationship.

Under what circumstances would you choose to end a friendship?

_____

_____

As you think about initiating a fierce conversation, or a series of conversations, with someone _before_ ending the relationship, prepare for that conversation. What would you say?

_____

_____

WANTS AND NEEDS

When we're in relationships where we're not getting what we want and need, we can feel very unfulfilled. Whether those wants and needs are physical, emotional, or spiritual, we may become unrecognizable to ourselves. The thriving, flourishing person we once were has left the building.

What are the things, in addition to love, that you want and need? List them here.

_____

_____

_____

MAKE IT HAPPEN

The responsibility for you getting your wants and needs met, ultimately, does not fall on your partner. It's on you. So if you have recognized ways that your needs are not being met, or parts of yourself that you've neglected, you have the opportunity to meet those needs and nurture those parts.

Maybe you felt most fully alive in a season when you were painting on canvas, but you haven't touched a paintbrush in a decade. Or maybe you know that you flourish when you stay physically active, but you haven't hiked or ridden your bike in months. (Roller-skating that once made your soul sing? Forget it. It's been years.) Perhaps you're someone who loves being around young people, and you stopped volunteering with a youth group after you got married. You are responsible for becoming, and continuing to be, the person you were created to be.

List five moments or activities in which you felt fully alive because you were being who you were created to be:

1. _____

2. _____

3. _____

4. _____

5. _____

Which one of those, or which version of one of those, can you choose to reprise in the next week? (For instance, if you're in your mideighties and you've got fragile, porous bones, roller-skating may be ill-advised. But you could visit the rink and cheer for the brand-new skaters.)

_____

_____

ONE THING

What is the one thing in this chapter that is most meaningful for you today? What idea or practice has the most traction in your life right now?

_____

_____

JUST DO IT

What is your next step? What is one practical way that you will implement this meaningful idea or practice in your life this week?

_____

_____

PART 3

The Eight Conversations of Fierce Love

11

Conversation 1: Do I Want This Relationship?

The first conversation to have—initially with yourself and then with your partner—is, "Do I want this relationship?" To be able to answer this, and to give your relationship the best chance of success, you need to ask if you are being the *you* that you were created to be. You being authentically you doesn't depend on whether or not you're in a relationship. It doesn't depend on whether you're living at the beach or in the mountains or in the city. It doesn't even depend on you having the dream house or the dream job or the dream family. You can be authentically who you really are in a variety of circumstances.

No one and no thing will ever be enough until *you* are enough, and you will never be enough until you are happy and successful in your own life. *Success*, of course, doesn't mean that you have the financial resources to buy an NBA team. Rather, we will be successful when there is complete alignment between who we are or wish to become and what we live. This is more important than most of us realize.

For this chapter, I'm asking you to take a pretty deep dive into *you*. I suggest that you carve out time and space to spend time with yourself. Treat yourself by creating your own personal retreat, ideally outside of your everyday environment.

LIVING WITH INTEGRITY

I mentioned in chapter 11 of *Fierce Love* that I found it pretty startling that the most important indicator of our health isn't lifestyle—smoking, drinking to excess, failure to exercise, etc.—but living with *integrity*. That means that who we are or wish to become matches the way we live. (Remember that list of qualities you hoped to find in another? Which ones were missing from your own life?) According to the study of psychoneuroimmunology, our immune system is literally weakened when there is a large gap between what we say we believe and how we actually behave. But when we make changes to live with integrity, our immune system is strengthened.

The areas of our lives where we might not be living with integrity include, but are not limited to

- diet,
- exercise,
- emotional health,
- faith,
- career,
- friendships,
- family relationships, and
- hobbies.

Is there an area, or are there areas, in which your life today is out of alignment with what you say you believe? What is out of whack right now? Be specific.

_____

_____

BEING WHO YOU WERE
MEANT TO BE

While the question "Am I being who I was meant to be?" sounds a little heady, and even peripheral to the more pressing issues of daily life, it is a critically important question to be asking.

As you consider the areas in which what you say you value doesn't match the way you're living, what can you do to correct these? (*Note:* Being specific will be more useful to you than being vague.)

I say this is important . . . _____

Yet what I do is . . . _____

I need to correct this by . . . _____

CHECK IN

If you're like most people, you don't often slow down to check in with yourself to determine where you are and how you're doing. To get you started, as you read the questions below, write down the first things that come to mind.

Are my interests and priorities shifting? If yes, from what to what?

_____

_____

What facets of myself have lain dormant or have never seen the light of day?

_____

_____

Is there an area I care about that is conspicuously absent from my life? If so, what is it?

_____

_____

To what degree am I realizing my full potential?

_____

_____

To what degree is there value and meaning in my life?

_____

_____

What am I called to do?

_____

_____

What activities have heart for me?

_____

_____

What's the most fun thing I'm going to do today?

_____

_____

If I am stressed, is this stress really worth it?

_____

_____

What one thing can I do to get more of what I want and need in my life?

_____

_____

KNOW YOUR
STUMP SPEECH

When political candidates of the nineteenth century shared with audiences what they were about, they'd stand on a stump and offer a speech outlining the key points of their message. I think that identifying who you are and where you're headed by writing your own "stump speech" is extremely valuable. It's basically answering the important questions, "Who am I and who do I wish to become? What do I want my life to be about?"

Note: If it helps you to peek at someone else's stump speech, you can return to chapter 11 in *Fierce Love* to read mine.

In your stump speech I'm inviting you to answer four questions:

1. Where am I going? (This is another way of saying, "What do I want? What matters to me? What's the ideal ending?")
2. Why am I going there?
3. Who is going with me? (Though it's about you, notice who's joining you on the journey.)
4. How will I get there?

Don't rush. Take all the time you need.

Having Conversation 1 with Your Partner: Do I Want This Relationship?

The ideal outcome of this conversation with your partner is clarifying what matters most to you both at this moment in time so that you have a deeper understanding, a deeper connection, assurance that your goals and values are aligned, and knowledge of how best to support each other. If you aren't aligned, you have things to think about, talk about further, and course correct if possible.

What you might say:

> I would like your feedback on something I've been thinking about. I came across four questions designed to help people clarify what matters most to them. I've written my answers to those questions, and I want to know if my answers seem authentic to you. Are they clear? Am I living up to what I've written? Do you see a change or shift I need to make? You up for that?

Assuming you get a yes, share your stump speech.

If your partner struggles to be helpful, perhaps say, "Please say more." Or "How could I say it so that it's closer to what you feel is true for me?" or "Where do you think I'm off track?"

As the conversation winds down, you could say, "I'd like to know how you would answer these questions for yourself. Maybe you could tell me sometime this weekend."

Listening well to each other's stump speech can clarify who you are individually as you work to nurture who you are together.

12

Conversation 2: Clarifying Conditions— Yours, Mine, Ours

Sometimes that quirky little habit that we found so endearing at the beginning of a relationship becomes that aggravating annoyance that eventually makes us want to stick a fork in our eye—or our partner's eye. Ideally you'll discover that your relationship can survive the chewing-while-eating noises, clothes dropped on the floor, disturbing wardrobe choices, and other sundry irritations that come with any relationship.

So the question I want you to be asking in this conversation is, "What conditions are essential for both of us to remain happy and committed in this relationship?"

ATTITUDE MATTERS

You know how it's more pleasant to be around an interesting person with a positive, upbeat attitude than someone stale who's often complaining and making negative comments? It can be difficult to be in relationship with people like this.

Would you say that your partner falls more on the side of being a Pollyanna or a Scrooge? (There's not a great measuring tool for this, so trust your gut.) Offer specific moments that support your assessment.

Would you say that you are more like Pollyanna or Scrooge? Offer specific moments that support your assessment.

_____

_____

_____

RECOGNIZING ENTRENCHED VICTIMS

Remember, when I use the term *entrenched victims*, I'm not describing people who have undergone something truly horrific and damaging. With this language I'm referring to those who seem to attract trouble and who, therefore, are chronically in need of rescuing, of sympathy. Bad things keep happening to them, and it's never their fault: *He did it to me. She's responsible. It's their fault.* Even though these people may be beautiful, lovable, and worthy, you want to be wary of being an enabler for folks who live as trouble magnets.

Are you in an enabling relationship with someone today? Explain.

_____

_____

_____

Are you willing to have the kind of fierce conversation I suggested in chapter 12 in _Fierce Love_ to deal with him or her? Reflect on this by writing how you might begin the conversation.

_____

_____

_____

KNOW YOUR DEAL BREAKERS

Though naming deal breakers can feel scary, it's actually more healthy for your relationship to identify what you will and will not tolerate.

What would be deal breakers in your relationship?

_____

_____

Does your partner know how you feel?

_____

_____

What are your partner's deal breakers?

_____

_____

HOW TO DISCOVER WHAT CAN AND CAN'T BE OVERLOOKED

Here are some conversation starters that can help you and a potential partner, or current one, discover what you can forgive, overlook, and live with and what are likely deal breakers. Take this conversation slowly. You'll know when the answers to these questions deserve further exploration.

Don't ask all of these questions in one conversation. That would feel like an interrogation! Work them into your conversations over time.

- On a scale of 1 to 10, how happy are you most of the time? If you're not happy, why not? Is your life working for you? If not, why not? What is essential to your happiness? What could prevent or has prevented or lessened your happiness?
- What are your core values? How do you define integrity? Tell me about a time when you recognized that you were out of integrity. What did you do?
- What do you want for yourself, for a (or our) relationship? (Children, career, goals, spirituality, money, sex, who does the cooking and cleaning, travel, ideal future? Of particular interest here is whether he or she views you as an equal.)
- What do you see as the differences in our personalities? What's good about these differences?

Could any of these cause a problem down the road? Do you feel it's workable for people who are very different to be together?

- Where are we similar? Are we both givers, takers? Spenders, savers? Athletic, not athletic? Love sports, don't love sports? Love sex, or could do without it? What's good about our similarities? Could any of our dissimilarities cause a problem?

- What is your primary love language? ("Do unto others" isn't always a good thing.)

- What are your conditions for remaining in a relationship (e.g., monogamy, truth, growth, integrity, kindness, generosity, happy in his or her own skin, must love dogs, etc.)?

- How will decisions be made? What if we disagree?

- On what topics might we compromise?

- How will money be handled? Yours, mine, ours?

- What are you committed to? (Animal rescue? Supporting the arts? Ending poverty?)

Remember, these questions are best approached gently and over time. Don't rush.

Having Conversation 2 with Your Partner: Clarifying Conditions— Yours, Mine, Ours

Tips for having this conversation and others:

1. It's important to slow this conversation down so it can find out what it wants and needs to be about.
2. If you aren't clear what your partner means (after all, words mean very different things to different people), ask for clarification. What I find myself saying in so many conversations is, "Say more about that. What does independence, success, spirituality, passion, career success, [fill in the blank] mean to you?"

What you might say:

I want us to create something beautiful and extraordinary together, so it always gets my attention when I hear about a couple parting because one or both of them were doing something that was intolerable to the other. Sometimes, it's not even something someone did, but rather an attitude or a strongly held belief.

It seems that love isn't truly unconditional, so I've thought about the conditions that for me are essential for our relationship to thrive.

I'd like to share them with you and get your feedback. Please ask questions if something I say isn't clear and also, importantly, if you foresee a problem.

Here are mine . . .

What are yours?

If you discover that your partner's conditions conflict with yours or you sense your partner isn't willing to respect your conditions or you are struggling with his or hers, don't start a fight! Just listen and take time to process. You might say:

Are you noticing that some of our conditions might be hard to fulfill? For example [fill in the blank]. I think it's important for both of us to give this some thought. Why don't we do that and circle back with each other this weekend (or tomorrow, or whatever makes sense). My hope is that we can resolve any difficulties because the conditions we've shared matter a great deal. Okay?

One of the things I love about this conversation is that, in preparing for it, you will become even clearer about what matters most to you.

13

Conversation 3: How Are We Really?

Because divorce is so prevalent in today's culture, it's likely that—regardless of your relationship status today—your life has been touched by divorce in some way. Maybe you have been divorced. Or maybe your parents are. Perhaps you've supported a friend or sibling enduring an arduous divorce. Around the world, the reason cited for almost half of divorces is incompatibility: qualities that are mutually antagonistic. For a relationship to thrive, it's important to face the ways individuals are different from one another and the ways those differences impact the relationship.

EVERY COUPLE HAS
INCOMPATIBILITIES

Since every person has unique emotional and physical wants and needs, as well as personality types, discovering how to love one another in the context of these differences is no small thing.

What are some of the differences you notice between who your partner is and who you are?

_____

_____

_____

Which of these differences interfere in your relationship?

_____

_____

_____

COMPROMISE IS KEY

In the face of differences, partners need to be committed to practicing what one article from *Psychology Today* calls "continual compromise."

In your relationship, is there a fair balance of compromise between partners? Offer specific examples to support your answer.

_____

_____

COMMUNICATION IS CRITICAL

A recent study in Australia named communication problems as the foremost issue that contributed to divorce.

Describe the type of communication you and your partner share (offering specific examples is most useful).

_____

_____

Which topics are most difficult to communicate about?

_____

_____

MISSING CONVERSATIONS

Remember in the introduction to *Fierce Love* how Louise ending the marriage took her husband, Tom, by surprise? It's not that Tom and Louise fought viciously over irresolvable issues. In fact, she hadn't even told him how deeply she was dissatisfied. She hadn't stated what she needed, hadn't made it clear how much those things mattered. Missing conversations can be just as dangerous as volatile ones. Some couples don't talk about financial matters. Others avoid discussing their sex life. Some avoid bringing up issues around addiction.

Is there an issue that matters to you today that you've not brought up with your partner?

_____

_____

You may recall that my image for a fierce conversation is a campfire. Build a campfire and people will be attracted to the smell of the wood smoke, the crackle, the warmth. They may add a log and begin to tell stories. Are you willing to build a campfire, sit beside the one you care for, and begin a conversation during which you are completely truthful?

THE WAY WE TELL THE TRUTH MATTERS

We've likely all been subjected to others who announce a blunt, hard, unkind truth that, if we're honest, we needed to hear. But there are helpful and unhelpful ways to tell the truth. Doing it well enriches the relationship in a way that deepens love rather than stalls or diminishes it.

The primary requirement for telling truth well is to describe reality from your perspective without laying blame. When we remove blame from the conversation, no one shuts down and we create possibilities that did not exist for us before.

If there's an issue on your heart that you need to discuss with your partner, on the lines below, practice introducing the conversation truthfully, without blame.

_____

_____

_____

 Having Conversation 3 with Your Partner: How Are We Really?

Here's a conversational model you can use to interrogate reality on any topic with your partner and with others. We will put it to work in a later chapter.

Conversational Model

Step 1: Name the topic you want to discuss.

If it's a problem, what is at the core of the problem? The problem named is the problem solved.

If you can't name it, you can't solve it. Be clear and concise. Perhaps you're thinking of changing careers or you'd like to move from the city to the country or you want to make a significant shift in lifestyle. Obviously, all of these things would involve and impact your partner, so don't keep your thoughts to yourself. Put them out there for discussion. Here is the flow:

> I've been thinking about . . .
> It's important to me because . . .
> Here are the options I've been
>   considering . . .
> If I had to make a decision or take action
>   today without your input, I'd choose . . .

You are acknowledging your reality and giving your partner an opportunity to learn more about how you see things.

Step 2: Invite your partner's perspective.

Now it's important to invite your partner to weigh in and to influence your thinking.

> I believe this would be a good thing, a good course of action. But you may see it differently. What are your thoughts? Feel free to challenge my thinking.

127

Because you don't know what you'll discover, this takes courage. Be sure to let your partner *actually* push back. Resist the temptation to defend yourself or strengthen your own case. Say, "Tell me more. Help me understand your thinking." And mean it.

Enriching Your Relationship

When you and your partner answer the questions below, no matter how close you are, you will likely learn things you didn't know, which is a great way to enrich the relationship.

Answer each question for yourself, share your answer with your partner, then ask your partner the same question. This needn't be a marathon. If a question leads to a long conversation, stop there. Take another question on another day.

The first section is about you as individuals. Discussing these will prime the pump for delving into the second set of questions, which is about your relationship.

What one experience do I most want to have in my life? What have I allowed to be in the way? What step could I take to move in that direction?

_____

_____

What do I most want to accomplish in my life? What could I do to advance this goal?

_____

_____

What activity have I always dreamed of doing that I haven't yet done?

_____

_____

If I could be mentored by anyone, living or dead, who would I select as my mentor? Why? What would I hope to learn?

_____

_____

What trait do I most deplore in myself? In others?

_____

_____

What is my greatest fear?

_____

_____

On what occasions do I lie?

_____

_____

What one or two words describe me best?

_____

_____

What is my motto?

_____

_____

Discuss these questions, and your answers to them, together.

What is the quality I value most in a partner, in you?

_____

_____

Is there a recent conversation where either of us felt we were avoiding the real issue? If not, hooray for us! If yes, what is the issue we avoided? Let's talk about it now.

_____

_____

How are we doing financially, given our long-term goals? Do we need to make any changes, adjustments? Are there steps we need to take?

_____

_____

If we were guaranteed honest responses from one another to any three questions, here's what I would ask. (Ask them, and vice versa. *Note:* If you're not ready to hear an honest answer, don't ask.)

_____

_____

What one thing could I do, you do, we do, that would enrich our relationship? (Be truthful, and encourage your partner to be truthful as well. Along the way, both of you will gain the understanding, respect, patience, forgiveness, and support that are essential to a healthy and happy relationship.)

_____

_____

_____

14

Conversation 4:
Getting Past "Honey,
I'm Home"

The conversation in this chapter is a "going
deeper" conversation. And it's one that can help you
achieve intimacy and connection better and quicker than
any other. Also, you can ask yourself these questions—or
invite a friend to ask them—to help you get to the root of
an issue on your plate, your mind, your heart.

So for this chapter, I'm going to welcome you to use
the process *first* with an issue you're facing personally.

Then, you can use the same questions to enter into a deep conversation with your partner.

THE CONVERSATION WITH YOURSELF: GETTING AT THE REAL ISSUE

1. Ask yourself what's most important.

This might sound like, "Self, when I think about everything I'm dealing with these days, everything that's on my plate, what's the most important thing on my mind?" If you don't know, ask yourself, "What would it be if I did know? I truly want to pay attention to what I'm wrestling with inside." ("I don't know" is too easy, too lazy, and rarely true. Commit to be better, braver, clearer.) When you're able to identify an issue, write it here:

_____

_____

_____

Now you've launched.

2. Ask questions about the issue.
What's going on relative to [fill in the blank]?

_____

_____

How long has it been going on?

_____

_____

What more can you add about this issue?

_____

_____

3. Clarify why this issue is important.
What result is this creating?

_____

_____

What is it affecting?

_____

_____

Who is it affecting?

_____

_____

Ask, "What else?" at least three times.

Then ask, "How is this currently impacting me?" This self-interrogation is one dripping with gentleness, kindness, and care. Treat yourself like the beloved and precious one you are.

How is this currently impacting me?

_____

_____

_____

Then go a bit deeper by asking, "When I consider everything I just described, what do I feel?" (*Note:* Not "How does this make me feel?")

_____

_____

Let's say you think, "Frustrated!" Write down why you feel frustrated. Or if you notice you feel "sad," write down why you feel sad.

_____

_____

After you've written down why you feel what you feel, answer, "What else do I feel?"

_____

_____

This next question will heighten your awareness about what may happen if things stay the same and, consequently, will motivate you to take action.

If nothing changes, what are the implications? What is likely to happen if nothing changes?

_____

_____

To notice any contributions you may have made to the issue, ask yourself, "Where are my fingerprints on this issue? How am I contributing to the problem?"

_____

_____

This next question points to the light at the end of this tunnel and propels you to take action.

Ask, "When this has been resolved and is no longer a problem, what difference will that make?"

_____

_____

Then ask, "What difference will that make for me?"

_____

_____

And finally, "When I contemplate that scenario, what do I feel?"

_____

_____

So that you move toward action, ask, "What's the next most useful step I can take to begin to resolve this issue?" If you don't know the answer, dig deeper by asking, "What would it be if I did know?"

_____

_____

What are you committed to doing, and when?

_____

_____

What will try to get in your way, and how will you get past that?

_____

_____

Having Conversation 4 with Your Partner: Getting Past "Honey, I'm Home"

Now it's time to have this conversation with your partner. These seven steps help you to move beyond a surface-level conversation to find a deeper connection with your partner. Be mindful to avoid these common mistakes:

- Doing most of the talking
- Giving advice
- Not inquiring about emotions
- Moving too quickly from question to question, which can morph into accusations

In this conversation, your job is to slow this conversation down so it can find out what it wants and needs to be about. In the process, your partner will feel heard, understood, loved, and genuinely helped and your relationship will be enriched.

STEP #1. If your partner tells you about an issue on his or her plate, you have the starting point for this conversation. If not, then ask, "When you think about everything you're dealing with these days, everything that's on your plate, what's the most important thing on your mind?"

If your partner says, "I don't know," ask, "What would it be if you did know? I ask because I truly want to know what you're dealing with these days."

Hopefully, your partner will give it some thought and say something like, "Well, I'm frustrated with a situation at work . . ." You're launched.

STEP #2. Ask questions about the issue: "What's going on relative to _____?" "How long has it been going on?" "Tell me more."

Sometimes it helps to tell your partner what

you think you're hearing, for example, "So, the issue is . . ." Don't be surprised if your partner says, "Well, not exactly." This is useful. You're helping to locate Grendel's mother if she's there.

STEP #3. Now it's time to further clarify why this issue is important. "What results is this creating? What else is it affecting? Who is it affecting?" Ask, "What else?" at least three times. Then ask, "How is this currently impacting you?"

This question conveys our care for our partner, our love, and often evokes an emotional response, which is a good thing. Go a bit deeper by asking, "When you consider everything you just described, what do you feel?" (**Note:** Not "How does this make you feel?")

Let's say they respond, "Frustrated!" Say, "Frustrated. Say more about that."

And after they've said more, ask, "What else do you feel?"

STEP #4. This next question will heighten your partner's awareness about what may happen if things stay the same and, consequently, will motivate your partner to take action. "If nothing changes, what are the implications?"

You could say, "Imagine it is a year from now and nothing has changed. What is likely to happen?" "What else?" "What's likely to happen for you if nothing changes?" Again, probe for emotion. "When you consider those possible outcomes, what do you feel?"

STEP #5. To help your partner recognize any contributions he or she may have made to the issue, ask: "When I'm faced with a problem, I can usually see my DNA on it somewhere, my contribution to the problem. Do you see your fingerprints anywhere on this issue?"

This is not the time to add your thoughts about where your partner went wrong, so don't comment on your partner's response, other than to say, "That's useful to recognize." Move on.

STEP #6. This next question points to the light at the end of this tunnel and propels your partner to take action. Ask: "When this has been resolved and is no longer a problem, what difference will that make?" Ask, "What else?" Then ask, "What difference will that make for you?" and finally, "When you contemplate that scenario, what do you feel?"

STEP #7. So that you don't leave your partner full of emotion with no place to go, ask, "What's the next most useful step you can take to begin to resolve this issue?" Again, if your partner says, "I don't know," ask, "What would it be if you did know?" Help your partner be better, braver, clearer. "What are you committed to do and when?" "What will try to get in your way and how will you get past that?"

15

Conversation 5: Let Me Count the Ways

If you've ever had someone notice the things about you that they appreciate and value, you know it feels fantastic. Specific affirmations—that go well beyond "Love ya! Mean it!"—are more meaningful than vague ones.

OFFER FEEDBACK

In *The One Minute Manager*, Ken Blanchard and Spencer Johnson suggest catching others in the act of doing something right and commenting on it: one minute or less of appreciation.

What is a recent moment when you saw your partner doing something really well? Something for which you're grateful? Something that touched you? On what could you offer positive feedback?

_____

_____

_____

BE SPECIFIC

Rather than telling your partner you're glad for what he does around the home or how she encourages you, *be specific.*

List particular instances when you valued who your partner is.

_____

_____

THE MODELING THAT MATTERS

My friend Jose is being intentional about the way he parents his daughter in the hopes that eventually she will look for a man who treats her well. The game changed for Jose when he learned that his daughter's model for "husband" wouldn't be the way he treated her but actually how he treated *his wife*.

When you were young, did your parents express their love and appreciation for each other in front of you?

_____

_____

Did they spend quality time with each other?

_____

_____

What did you learn from your parents' relationship?

_____

_____

How have you seen that learning express itself in previous relationships and in this one?

_____

_____

WHAT TO DO WITH WHAT YOU'VE SEEN MODELED

When we don't pay attention to what we saw modeled about intimate relationships as children, we are likely to repeat the patterns we witnessed. But when we are intentional about noticing our early experience, we can choose how we will behave as adults.

What about the relationship between your earliest caregivers is worth replicating?

_____

_____

_____

What about the relationship between your earliest caregivers do you want to do differently?

_____

_____

_____

Specifically, what are you doing differently?

_____

_____

_____

Having Conversation 5 with Your Partner: Let Me Count the Ways

While this conversation of appreciation might be one that you schedule on your calendar to remind you to tell your partner the specific things about him or her for which you're grateful, it's also one that works well on the fly.

Did you roll into the driveway while your partner was mowing the grass? Tell her you appreciate how she contributes to the household economy. When you let your partner know that you'd been feeling emotionally low, did he or she listen really well and ask exactly the right questions? Tell him how much you value him. Or on the day of the big meeting at work, did you come home to find dinner was waiting for you? Let your partner know what it is that you value and appreciate about him or her.

There are a variety of ways to have this "Let Me Count the Ways" conversation, so choose which one makes the most sense for your relationship.

Plan a Time to Share

When you want to be intentional about this conversation, put it on your calendar to make sure it happens.

Schedule Regular "Warm Seat" Moments

Once a month, you and your partner can take turns being in the "warm seat." The one in the warm seat has sixty seconds to share what he or she feels they bring to the relationship. Then, the partner shares, specifically, what it is they appreciate about that person. Be precise, thoughtful. Remember, the person in the warm seat can only say one thing in response to the affirmations he or she receives: *Thank you.*

Express Your Appreciation in the Moment

When you're enjoying who your partner is and who you are together, let your partner know. In that moment. Maybe you're cuddling on the couch. Maybe you're driving home from a holiday with your in-laws. Or maybe you're watching your child's soccer game. In the moment you notice your appreciation for your partner, let him or her know.

Share Your Appreciation Without Words

Offer a glance, a smile, a hug, a kiss, a massage, a cuddle to let your partner know you value him or her.

Write Your Appreciation

The list a man created of the things he loved about me was a wonderful gift. It was deeply personal, and he'd clearly given it a lot of thought. Consider sharing a written list with your partner of what you appreciate about him or her.

16

Conversation 6: It's Not You, It's Me

While it would be great if we could pair up with partners who are flawless, it turns out that there are no perfect people. Each relationship includes two imperfect people. And relationships don't survive unless we're willing to tolerate imperfections in our partners and also acknowledge that we have a few of our own.

FAILING TO ACKNOWLEDGE
AND APOLOGIZE FOR
OUR IMPERFECTIONS

It can be hard to admit we're wrong, especially when our words or actions have potentially harmed our relationship.

How easy or difficult is it for you to acknowledge and apologize for your imperfections? (Offer specific examples.)

_____

_____

In your opinion, how easy or difficult does it seem for your partner to acknowledge and apologize for his or her imperfections? (Offer specific examples.)

_____

_____

APOLOGIZING TOO FREQUENTLY ISN'T HELPFUL

While it takes awareness and courage to offer a sincere apology, apologizing too frequently, and too vociferously, can feel irritating.

Have you known anyone who *over*-apologizes for that which is not his or hers to own?

_____

_____

How did you experience this person? What harm was done by his or her over-apologizing?

_____

_____

PAUSE BEFORE SPEAKING

Inspector Gamache, of Louise Penny's murder mysteries, offers wise counsel to those he mentors. Before speaking, he offers, one should ask three questions:

- Is it true?
- Is it kind?
- Does it need to be said?

What would be different about your own speech if you practiced these three?

_____

_____

FOUR SENTENCES WE MUST LEARN AND MEAN

Gamache also shared four things we must learn to say and mean:

- I don't know.
- I need help.
- I'm sorry.
- I was wrong.

Which of these sentences comes to your lips with the most ease?

_____

_____

Which of these sentences is the most difficult for you to spit out?

_____

_____

Can you say why?

_____

_____

LEARN HOW NOT TO APOLOGIZE

As you consider the nature of poor apologies, which aren't really apologies at all, here's what to avoid:

- If you're in the wrong, don't say, "I'm sorry you feel that way."
- Don't demand an apology.
- Don't ruin an apology by tacking on an excuse.
- Don't apologize for your emotions (e.g., "I'm sorry I'm crying").
- Don't blame others for your wrongs.

As you consider your own personal history of apologies, which of these are temptations for you?

_____

_____

Having Conversation 6 with Your Partner: It's Not You, It's Me

The conversation where you apologize to your partner is one of the most important conversations you can have. In fact, it can be a relationship saver!

If you're ready to offer a sincere apology to your partner, here are some key markers, in no particular order, of a good one:

- I'm sorry for _____.
  (Specifying your wrong is more helpful than being vague. "I blew it, and here's how . . .")
- I hear you.

- I see how my words or behavior affected you.
- Here's what I've done to rectify my wrong . . .
- I'd like to do it differently next time.
- Will you forgive me?

Take a moment to write out the apology you need to share with your partner.

_____

_____

_____

17

Conversation 7: It's Not Me, It's You

If a problem exists in a relationship, it exists whether we talk about it or not. If it's the kind of problem that has the potential to damage or end the relationship, that conversation is essential. And yet when someone inquires, "Would you like some feedback?" we likely do not! No one *asks* before they let us know how attractive or smart or kind we are. Rather, we balk because we know that people typically ask permission to offer the kind of feedback that stings. Yet feedback has the power to resurrect a dying relationship.

OFFERING FEEDBACK DOESN'T NEED TO BE COMFORTABLE

If we're the person who's considering offering feedback to a partner about something he or she has done that concerns us, we likely feel a certain degree of discomfort. But if our relationship is to flourish, we need to make its success more important than comfort.

Are you in the habit of offering feedback to your partner? Why or why not?

_____

_____

_____

Is your partner in the habit of offering feedback to you? Why or why not?

_____

_____

_____

NOTICE HOW YOU
OFFER FEEDBACK

A lot of us have room to grow when it comes to offering feedback to our partners. Recall the last time you were upset with your partner.

What did you say to him/her?

_____

_____

What was the tone of your voice? Did you raise your voice? Did you curse?

_____

_____

What was the expression on your face?

_____

_____

163

What would it have been like to have been on the receiving end of that moment?

_____

_____

Would you have fallen into the traditional mode of fight or flight or would you have invited a conversation with your partner so that you could understand why your partner was unhappy or upset?

_____

_____

Would you have felt loved, cherished, valued?

_____

_____

(To keep you honest, would your partner disagree with any of your answers?)

FEEDBACK IS HELPFUL WHEN WE'D LIKE SOMETHING TO CHANGE

Feedback is when we let our partner know that something they've said or done concerns us. We point out something and ask what's going on. We let our partner know that we didn't love what they did or said and we'd prefer they didn't do it again.

Here are the types of situations that can benefit from offering feedback to our partners:

- It's never happened before and I don't think my partner was aware that he or she did it.
- I see a pattern that could become a problem later on and want to share it with my partner so that he or she has an opportunity to course correct.
- It happened once—I do not necessarily have an expectation that my partner changes, but rather I want to make sure he or she sees it from my perspective.
- A mistake was made and it's important to share insights on what could have been done better.

Has there been an issue in your relationship where one partner has offered the other feedback? What happened?

_____

_____

_____

Is there an issue today in which offering your partner feedback could benefit the relationship? Describe the issue.

_____

_____

_____

CONFRONTATION IS NECESSARY WHEN AN ISSUE *MUST* CHANGE

When an issue is more serious, we need to do more than offer feedback. We need to be willing to confront our partner. When something *must* change, it's time for a confrontation.

Here are the types of situations that can benefit from confrontation:

- There is a pattern of similar behavior. I've said something and nothing is changing or it is not changing quickly enough.
- My partner has done something and even once is too much.
- It keeps happening, and now it is affecting our relationship.
- Mistakes keep being made and there is an underlying issue that needs to be explored and corrected to prevent further damage to our relationship.

Has there been an issue in your relationship where one partner has confronted the other? What happened?

_____

_____

_____

Is there an issue today in which confronting your partner could benefit the relationship? Describe the issue.

_____

_____

_____

_____

_____

THE CRUCIBLE IS RESILIENT

A crucible is a strong, resilient vessel in which profound change can safely take place. When we act as crucibles for conversations—with our partners, with family, with friends, with ourselves—our job is to *hold* and not drop what is poured in under extreme heat. In this way we're able to discuss what needs discussing no matter how challenging the topic and no matter how fragile and vulnerable either party may be feeling at the time.

How difficult or easy is it for you to hold steady in these fierce conversations? How do you behave in these conversations? Say more about that.

_____

_____

_____

WE TELL OURSELVES STORIES

When Jim's wife, Brenda, forgot to do what she'd promised, he made up a story: "If my wife loved me, she would have done what I'd requested." But he might also have told himself another story about what happened: "My wife loves me, but she was focused on something else and forgot my request."

Have you told yourself a story about your partner that caused sadness, anger, or pain? Explain.

_____

_____

What argument are you waging? (What's the story you're telling?)

_____

_____

What are you trying to be right about?

_____

_____

If you win your argument, what's the prize?

_____

_____

TELL A BETTER STORY

The challenge is to catch ourselves in the act of making up a story about *why* our partner did or said what he or she did or said, especially if we are convinced the story we are telling ourselves is true. We need to ask ourselves,

"Could I be wrong?" The stories we tell ourselves make us happy or they make us angry, resentful, sad, or anxious. What if those stories are bogus?

As you consider the story you've told yourself about your partner that has caused you anger, resentment, sadness, or anxiety, could you be wrong? Reflect on that possibility.

_____

_____

Having Conversation 7 with Your Partner: It's Not Me, It's You

Begin by providing context for this feedback. _When, where,_ and _what_ did you see? Describe what happened or what they did just like a video camera would capture it, without using loaded words. _What_ did they do or say that you feel is important to give them feedback about? _What_ did you observe?

Then ask, "Can you tell me what was going on?"

Your partner may apologize and give you a perfectly reasonable answer. But what if he or she doesn't see the problem?

Now it's time to briefly (let me emphasize "briefly") describe the impact for him or her, for you, for your relationship. *Why* you brought this up.

You could say,

> I got the impression that something else was more important than our time together. When I asked you about the call, you dismissed it in a tone that felt contemptuous. I felt shut down, shut out. The result, whether you intended it or not, is that I'm not eager to spend time with you right now. I'd say that's a problem.

This isn't easy! But it's worth it.

18

Conversation 8: I Love You, but I Don't Love Our Life Together

There are a number of reasons that unhappy people stay together. Sometimes it's for the children. It may be because one partner is financially dependent on the other. One or both partners might be convicted, spiritually, that they need to honor their marriage vows. It also might be a matter of fear: fearing being alone, fearing not finding another partner, or fearing a loss of identity. And other times we just ignore how bad a situation really is.

Because you once loved this person deeply, enough to commit to him or her, it's worth giving your relationship the attention and care it deserves.

This is the conversation you want to have with your partner when one of you can see that something in your relationship *must* change or the relationship is in serious trouble.

WE MAY HAVE FEARS ABOUT HAVING A REAL, HARD CONVERSATION

Our fears about initiating a hard conversation might include:

- ☐ A confrontation could escalate the problem rather than resolve it.
- ☐ I could lose the relationship.
- ☐ Confronting the behavior could force an outcome for which I am not prepared.
- ☐ I could incur retaliation.
- ☐ I may not be taken seriously.
- ☐ The cure could be worse than the disease.

☐ I could be met with irrationality or emotional outbursts.

☐ I could discover that I am part of the problem.

Now put a check mark beside the *three concerns* at the top of your list for avoiding the conversation that needs to happen.

WHAT WE SAY AND *HOW* WE SAY IT MATTERS

What we say is important. And *how* we say it is important. The failure of conversations can often be attributed to the delivery as much as the content!

Until now, have you been able to offer a simple, powerful, clear approach when you bring up a difficult issue? Are you able to remain grounded, calm, and clear? If not, what does your style of communication, in confrontation, sound like?

_____

_____

What about your partner? What is his or her delivery like when confronting?

_____

_____

AVOID COMMON MISTAKES

As you consider the common mistakes people make when confronting a partner, put a check beside the ones that you've been tempted to use, or have used, in the past (return to chapter 18 in _Fierce Love_ if you need a refresher on what each sounds like):

- ☐ Blaming
- ☐ Name-calling, labeling
- ☐ Attaching global weight to tip-of-the-iceberg stuff
- ☐ Threatening, intimidating
- ☐ Exaggerating
- ☐ Pointing to your partner's failure to communicate, assuming a position of superiority, and believing your partner is clearly inferior
- ☐ Saying, "If I were you . . ."
- ☐ Gunnysacking, bringing up a lot of old baggage

☐ Assassinating your partner in public
☐ Asking, "Why did you do that?" instead of "What were you trying to do?"
☐ Making blatantly negative facial expressions
☐ Layering your interpretation on something your partner has said or done
☐ Being unresponsive, refusing to speak, leaving the room

WHO'S NOT READY?

We can at times convince ourselves that our partner isn't ready to have the hard conversation. And yet what most people confess is that it's we ourselves who can't handle it, who aren't ready. And yet if you know something must change, then know that it is you who must change it.

If you have recognized a problem in your relationship and have not yet broached the conversation with your partner, reflect on why you've not moved forward.

_____

_____

CLAMMING UP AND BLOWING UP

A lot of us haven't seen confrontation done well. We don't know how to initiate it, and we don't know how to receive it. If we don't know how to navigate confrontation when we're on the receiving end of it, we'll be tempted to clam up or blow up.

When confronted, are you more likely to clam up or blow up? Describe a conversation when you remember having this response, and then describe how you might have responded differently.

_____

_____

_____

RESPONDING TO CONFRONTATION

Because you and your partner are human, it's possible each of you might naturally respond to confrontation in one of three unhelpful ways: deny, deflect, defend.

- "Deny" might sound like, "I don't know what you're talking about."
- "Defend" might sound like, "I'm doing my part. I can't believe you're making me the bad guy."
- "Deflect" might sound like, "Well what about *you*?!"

Which, if any, of these three describe the way you're naturally tempted to respond to confrontation?

_____

_____

_____

Name a particular instance of confrontation with your partner, note your response, and then write how you might have responded differently.

_____

_____

_____

Having Conversation 8 with Your Partner: I Love You, but I Don't Love Our Life Together

When something must change in your relationship, the conversation you and your partner must have has three parts: opening statement, interaction, and resolution.

Opening Statement

If there is a confrontation that has your name on it, if love is no longer being served, write a draft of your sixty-second invitation to the conversation, and then rehearse it aloud.

For example:

- "I want to talk with you about the effect your angry outbursts are having on our relationship."
- "I am [emotion], because there is a lot at stake. If nothing changes . . ."
- "I recognize that I [your contribution to the problem], and for this, I apologize."

- "I want us to resolve the effect that
  _____ is having on _____.
  Please tell me what you are thinking and
  feeling."

- _____

- _____

Say it out loud, see how it feels. Does it ring true? Does it evoke emotion in you? Time it and edit it so that you don't go over sixty seconds and so that you have made it as clear and compelling as possible.

Now, screw your courage to the sticking place, as Shakespeare put it, and start the conversation.

Interaction

After you've offered your opening statement, go into listening mode. When your partner responds, say, "I want to understand your thinking, so please say more about that."

Resolution

The third part of this conversation is resolution. When your partner feels that you fully understand and acknowledge his or her view of reality, move toward resolution, which includes an agreement about what is to happen next.

19

Love After Love

If your relationship has been suffering, you likely want to do whatever you can to revive it.

When the original blazing campfire of love has been extinguished and it seems only ashes remain, we want to make sure we've done our part to nurture the health of the relationship.

I'VE DONE MY PART

Put a check mark beside each marker to indicate the efforts you've invested in the relationship (***Note:*** It's not a competition. This is just for you!):

- ☐ I understand that the conversation *is* the relationship.
- ☐ I let my partner know what I appreciate about him or her.
- ☐ I have expressed gratitude, given and received feedback, apologized when I was in the wrong.
- ☐ I have listened deeply when my partner was wrestling with a problem.
- ☐ I clarify conditions, stay current with my partner, do my best to connect with my partner at a deep level, and work to ensure my own life is working well.
- ☐ I've confronted the issue at the heart of the problems in the relationship.

Notice those efforts where you *haven't* placed a check mark. How will you invest in one or more of those?

_____

_____

_____

HAS THE END COME?

For some there comes a day when the pain of the relationship is too great, when we've tried and there just isn't
anything more to say, when we look at the future and
the person we are with isn't in it. Such a sad moment.

**Below, list and reflect on the reasons this may be
the end of your relationship.**

_____

_____

_____

**Now list and reflect on the reasons this may not
be the end of your relationship.**

_____

_____

_____

HAVE YOU ADDRESSED
THE ISSUE?

You may recall from chapter 19 in *Fierce Love* that on their Hawaiian vacation, Karen knew that her relationship with Mark was over. I suspect Mark may have been blindsided by the breakup because Karen hadn't done the work along the way to offer him feedback about his behavior.

Before ending a relationship prematurely, make sure you've done your part:

Have you offered feedback to your partner about the specific things that are bothering you?

_____

_____

If yes, and your partner kept deliberately doing things to upset you, have you confronted your partner, clarifying what was likely to happen if your partner continued behaving in that way?

_____

_____

CONSIDER A NEW POSSIBILITY

I'm convinced that being deeply happy can look a variety of ways. For some, this will be within the context of a committed relationship. And others will find deep happiness outside of a relationship.

Have you considered the possibility that you might be most satisfied outside of a committed relationship?

_____

_____

If so, and you did not or do not have a partner, what do you imagine would—or does!—bring you joy?

_____

_____

With or without a partner, what will you be sure to include in your life to make sure you are flourishing? (These are starters to help you brainstorm. Add your own!)

- ☐ Friends
- ☐ Family
- ☐ Season tickets to the theater
- ☐ Volunteering as a docent at the art museum
- ☐ Visiting Loch Ness or other places of interest
- ☐ Going out and mingling with others
- ☐ Devoting time and energy to being a better friend/parent/grandparent
- ☐ Taking a class
- ☐ Volunteering in civic organizations
- ☐ Spending time helping an aging neighbor
- ☐ _____
- ☐ _____

ONE THING

What is the one thing in this chapter that is most meaningful for you today? What idea or practice has the most traction in your life right now?

_____

_____

JUST DO IT

What is your next step? What is one practical way that you will implement this meaningful idea or practice in your life this week?

_____

_____

Conclusion

Putting Fierce Love to Work

Although a lot of us invest time, money, and energy into our careers, our appearance, our education, our homes, our financial portfolios, and more, we eventually discover that these aren't what truly satisfy. Our most valuable currency is relationship, emotional capital, which we acquire or squander one conversation at a time.

INVEST IN FRIENDSHIPS

The person you are most meant to love, to connect with at a deep level, will always be yourself. I also want to encourage you to pause to consider the friendships in your life today.

As you think about your life, who are the friends who mean the most to you?

_____

_____

What are you and your friends contributing to one another?

_____

_____

What do you talk about?

_____

_____

What is the tone of your conversations?

_____

_____

How do you feel as a result of your friendships?

_____

_____

Is this what you want for yourself? Why or why not?

_____

_____

If you are spending time with someone who gossips, judges, criticizes, whose life has basically flatlined, reflect on why.

_____

_____

Are you the one who gossips, judges, criticizes, whose life has flatlined? Reflect on why.

_____

_____

Are you satisfied with these friendships? Why or why not?

_____

_____

If you're not satisfied with your friendships, make new friends.

ARE YOUR FRIENDSHIPS FLOURISHING?

As you read through the qualities of genuine human connectivity below, write down the name of a friend who embodies each quality. (Feel free to write down more than one name for each.)

- practicing empathy
- being understanding
- being transparent
- asking fact-finding questions, showing curiosity
- paying attention to the whole being
- having compassion once you know the story
- being yourself, authentic, genuine

- going deep and showing vulnerability
- having an open mind
- not pushing your own personal agenda
- being clear and direct, no sugarcoating
- responding appropriately
- avoiding us versus them
- acknowledging human imperfection and human experience

BE FIERCE DAILY

When you really start listening, you'll begin to notice opportunities to be fierce. As you notice yourself avoiding a topic, changing the subject, holding back, telling little (or big) lies, you'll start to see opportunities to be fierce. In these moments I want you to stop and take a deep breath. Then, come out from behind yourself into the conversation and make it real.

In these pages you've given a good deal of consideration to what good conversations sound like in romantic relationships. But every relationship in your life will benefit when you choose to engage in fierce conversations.

As you consider your friendships, in what ways do you need to come out from behind yourself to be more real in conversations? (Be specific.)

_____

_____

_____

As you consider your professional relationships, in what ways do you need to come out from behind yourself to be more real in conversations? (Be specific.)

_____

_____

_____

As you consider your relationships with members of your family who don't live in your household, in what ways do you need to come out from behind yourself to be more real in conversations? (Be specific.)

_____

_____

_____

Are there other relationships in your life that can benefit from fierce conversations? Which people and in what ways?

_____

_____

_____

TAKE THE NEXT STEP

If you try to do everything to improve your relationship at once, you'll likely find yourself frustrated and over-whelmed. It will be tempting to give up. You are most likely to succeed if you release your drive to do every-thing and instead choose to do the *next* thing.

Because relationships happen one conversation at a time, what's the next conversation you need to have with your partner?

_____

_____

BE WHO YOU REALLY ARE

The key to your happiness doesn't lie in another person. It resides with you. What practical steps will you take to become the person you really are? Maybe you'll write that book that you've held in your heart. Maybe you'll paint the painting. Climb the mountain. Run the race.

What will you commit to pursue to be the person you were made to be?

_____

_____

ONE THING

What is the one thing in this chapter that is most meaningful for you today? What idea or practice has the most traction in your life right now?

_____

_____

JUST DO IT

What is your next step? What is one practical way that you will implement this meaningful idea or practice in your life this week?

_____

_____

Acknowledgments

Bucketfuls of gratitude to Daniel Ladinsky, whose translations of Hafiz's poems in *The Gift* are so beautiful. Thank you, Danny, for allowing me to share two of them in this book. And to William Baer for "Letter of Resignation," Robert Francis for "Summons," and the many authors I've quoted in this book. You said it far better than I could.

More bucketfuls to friends who allowed me to tell their stories.

Thanks to Dianna Kokoszka, who invited me to lead the very first Fierce Love session for several hundred Keller Williams people in Austin, Texas, years ago. Their wholehearted response persuaded me that this book had an audience.

Thanks to my editors, Jen Gingerich, Margot

Starbuck, and Brigitta Nortker at Thomas Nelson/HarperCollins for making this a better book. I am not always as clear as I'd like to be, and you three helped solve that problem. And oh, the philosophical debates we had! So useful!

Finally, thank you to Raoul Davis and Leticia Gomez with the Ascendant Group for agenting this book and getting the word out, and to Ed Beltran, Paul Stabile, Luis Gonzales, and my supportive fierce tribe for excusing me from my regular responsibilities so I could focus on writing and developing our online Fierce Love course: FierceInc.com/Resources/Fierce-Love/.

Oh, and I should thank the men in my life with whom I found a thousand wrong ways to have challenging conversations until we finally got it right. Whew! And also my family: it isn't always easy living with someone who doesn't tiptoe around issues. On the other hand, I'd like to believe I've contributed to my granddaughters' confidence in navigating their relationships. They're pretty spectacular, if I do say so myself.

Every kindness,
Susan Scott
July 2021

Notes

Chapter 2: Gradually Then Suddenly

12   "Gradually and then suddenly": Ernest Hemingway, *The Sun Also Rises: The Hemingway Library Edition* (New York: Simon & Schuster, 2016), 109.

16   "It is important": William Stafford, "A Ritual to Read to Each Other," in *The Way It Is: New and Selected Poems* (Minneapolis: Graywolf, 1998), 76.

Chapter 4: Crossing the Bold Line

30   "In real love": Margaret Anderson, quoted in Stephen Spender, "European Places, People and Events," *New York Times Book Review*, November 18, 1979, 1, https://www.nytimes.com/1979/11/18/archives/european-places-people-and-events-flanner.html.

Notes

Chapter 5: What Isn't *Fierce Love?*

44   "four conversational signs": J. M. Gottman and R.
W. Levenson, "A Two-Factor Model for Predicting
When a Couple Will Divorce: Exploratory Analyses
Using 14-Year Longitudinal Data," *Family Process* 41,
no. 1 (March 2002): 83–96, https://onlinelibrary.wiley
.com/doi/10.1111/j.1545-5300.2002.40102000083.x.

Chapter 13: Conversation 3: How Are We Really?

123 "continual compromise": Alex Lickerman, "The
Real Reason Couples Decide They're Incompatible,"
Psychology Today, February 3, 2013, https://www
.psychologytoday.com/us/blog/happiness-in-world
/201302/the-real-reason-couples-decide-theyre
-incompatible.

123 "A recent study in Australia": Ilene Wolcott and
Jody Hughes, "Towards Understanding the Reasons for
Divorce" (working paper, Australian Institute of Family
Studies, Melbourne, June 1999), https://aifs.gov.au
/sites/default/files/publication-documents/WP20.pdf.

Chapter 16: Conversation 6: It's Not You, It's Me

156 "Inspector Gamache": Louise Penny, *A Better Man*
(New York: Minotaur Books, 2019), 184.

Conclusion

194 "practicing empathy": Susan Scott, *Fierce Conversations: Achieving Success at Work and in Life, One Conversation at a Time*, rev. ed. (New York: New American Library, 2004), 8–9.

About the Author

Susan Scott is a *New York Times* bestselling author and leadership development architect who for two decades has enabled top executives worldwide to engage in vibrant dialogue with one another, with their employees, and with their customers. She pioneered the process of fierce conversations that has touched the lives of millions of people, and now she's freshly applying these ideas to our romantic relationships. Susan lives in Medina, Washington.

Accompanying book available now!